The New Novello Choral Edition
NOVELLO HANDEL EDITION

General Editor   Donald Burrows

Four Coronation Anthems
(HWV 259, 258, 260, 261)

Four Anthems for the Coronation of King George II and Queen Caroline, 1727

SSAATBB (SATB) Chorus and Orchestra

Edited by Donald Burrows and Damian Cranmer

Vocal score

ISBN: 978-0-7119-9589-5

NOVELLO

part of **WiseMusic**Group

EXCLUSIVELY DISTRIBUTED BY
HAL•LEONARD®

Contact us:
Hal Leonard
7777 West Bluemound Road
Milwaukee, WI 53213
Email: info@halleonard.com

In Europe, contact:
Hal Leonard Europe Limited
42 Wigmore Street
Marylebone, London, W1U 2RY
Email: info@halleonardeurope.com

In Australia, contact:
Hal Leonard Australia Pty. Ltd.
4 Lentara Court
Cheltenham, Victoria, 3192 Australia
Email: info@halleonard.com.au

GEORGE FRIDERIC HANDEL
Four Coronation Anthems
(HWV 259, 258, 260, 261)

APPROXIMATE DURATIONS

Let thy hand be strengthened	9 minutes
Zadok the Priest	6 minutes
The King shall rejoice	11 minutes
My heart is inditing	12 minutes

INSTRUMENTATION

2 oboes
2 bassoons
3 trumpets
timpani
strings
Continuo (organ and/or harpsichord)

Let thy hand be strengthened does not require trumpets and timpani.
Zadok the Priest is the only anthem with two independent bassoon parts.

Music setting by Stave Origination

Orchestral material is available on hire from the Publisher. Permission to reproduce from the Preface of this edition must be obtained from the Publisher.

CONTENTS

PREFACE

Handel's four Coronation Anthems were composed for, and first performed at, the coronation of King George II and Queen Caroline, which took place in Westminster Abbey on 11 October 1727. The main outlines of the coronation service and its liturgy were well established by tradition and precedent, though varying circumstances made each event individual. The 1727 coronation was the first since 1685 of a King and Queen consort, and it saw the restoration to the service of the Holy Communion element which had been omitted in 1685. It was also only the second coronation of a King of Great Britain: the previous coronation, of King George I (George II's father) in 1714, had been the first one following the Act of Union. King George II was approaching his 44th birthday, and Queen Caroline had just passed hers; both were of the same generation as George Frideric Handel, who was two years younger. The coronation seems to have been one of the major social events in London during the first half of the eighteenth century, and had a lustre that had been lacking in the previous two coronations, of Queen Anne and King George I. Handel's anthems must have contributed substantially to the grandeur and the memorability of the occasion. Handel had made his mark in London with the Te Deum and Jubilate that he composed for the public Thanksgiving Service for the Peace of Utrecht in 1713: the coronation anthems were his second essay in the grand ceremonial style that was his original, and subsequently very influential, contribution to the course of English church music. With these works he shifted the harmonic and declamatory musical language to a new basis, as decisively as Purcell and his contemporaries had done in terms of their own style in the last quarter of the previous century.

The precise timetable under which Handel composed the anthems is not known, and he did not date the autograph. It is possible that his involvement in the coronation service brought with it some difficulties in his relationship with other participants, which went unreported because the arrangements for the music were but one part of the elaborate proceedings that the event involved. King George I died on 11 June 1727, in the course of a journey to Hanover: he was buried abroad, so there was no state funeral in London. The principal English-born composer of the Chapel Royal, William Croft, died on 14 August: he had completed a new organ-accompanied verse anthem, *Give the King thy judgements* on 13 July, perhaps as a contribution to the anticipated coronation, but he seems to have been taken ill fairly soon afterwards. Croft had composed the principal orchestrally-accompanied anthem for King George I's coronation in 1714, and would presumably have had some role in 1727 if he had lived. Handel may well have heard Croft's anthem at the 1714 coronation, to which he did not contribute any music himself, in spite of the good impression that he had made with the 'Utrecht' music the year before.

Between the two coronations, however, Handel's situation had changed in two important respects. In 1723 he had been appointed a Composer of the Chapel Royal, not on the regular establishment but apparently as a kind of composer laureate who produced occasional music for Chapel Royal services attended by the King - specifically for the Sunday services marking the King's safe return from visits to Hanover. Although he qualified for the receipt of Royal pensions, Handel was not in a position to hold conventional court office owing to his foreign status, but in February 1727 he had moved a step closer when his name was added to a Parliamentary Bill of naturalisation. The Royal assent to this had been one of George I's last official acts before leaving for Hanover, but the timing must have been a coincidence, for when he left England, the King appeared to be in good health and news of his subsequent death was greeted with surprise. Thus, as it happened, by the summer of 1727 Handel was better placed than before to compose the principal music for the coronation. On September 14 a London newspaper reported that Handel had been 'appointed' to compose the coronation music,[1] and we may suppose that he had begun the composition by then: there were public rehearsals in the Abbey on 6 and 9 October. Maurice Greene was appointed to Croft's former office in the Chapel Royal, and may perhaps have expected to have contributed some music of his own but, according to an anecdote recorded later by King George III, Handel was the King's exclusive choice for the occasion.

The anthem texts that Handel set had been traditional elements within the coronation liturgy, though the precise selection of verses and details of the wording varied. The anthem words were apparently regarded as being a sufficiently integral part of the liturgy that they were included in the order of service that was prepared under the direction of the Archbishop of Canterbury, approved by the Privy Council on 20 September and then printed. Handel's texts do not conform exactly to those in this document, perhaps because he had already written the music by 20 September. Charles Burney reported a story that, when Handel was presented with the texts, he reacted by saying 'I have read my bible very well, and shall chuse for myself'. More significantly, there are grounds for doubting that Handel's anthems were performed at exactly the places in the service that are designated by the printed order of service. A handwritten record of details of the music performed at the coronation service, entered into the 'Cheque Book' of the Chapel Royal, indicates that, while *Zadok the Priest* and *My heart is inditing* were performed at the obviously appropriate moments of the Anointing and the Queen's Coronation, respectively, *Let thy hand be strengthened* was performed early in the service at the Recognition and *The King shall rejoice* at the Crowning: the Archbishop's order of service has *The King shall rejoice* at the Recognition and *Let thy hand be strengthened* later on at the 'Inthronisation', with a completely different text (*Praise the Lord, O Jerusalem*) for the Crowning. For this edition, the anthems are presented in the order given in the Chapel Royal manuscript, which may be a better guide to what happened on the day. This order in any case puts the anthems at moments in the service which are appropriate both to their texts and the nature of the musical settings that they received. It is possible that confusion about the order of the anthems was even a feature of the service itself, and that for the first of Handel's anthems one group of performers set off with *The King shall rejoice* while another group began *Let thy hand be strengthened*: whatever the cause, the Archbishop of Canterbury wrote in his copy of the order of service at that point 'The Anthem in Confusion: all irregular in the music'. Without modern facilities for the careful management of ceremonial state occasions, it is not surprising that there were imperfections of communication: previous experience could not cover every eventuality for infrequently-held events such as coronation services, especially when they involved innovations such as an unprecedently large group of musicians. In 1761, at the time of the following coronation, William Boyce described Handel's music as 'the First Grand Musical Performance in the Abbey' and contemporary reports told of prodigious numbers of performers: one newspaper account of a rehearsal talked of 40 voices and an orchestra of 160, and another said that the performers would be 'Italian voices and above 100 of the best musicians'. These may have been exaggerated, but the orchestra probably outnumbered the singers, and the Court records noted payments for 57 orchestral musicians and about 14 singers to supplement the musicians of the Court establishments. Whether London's pool of English singers from the ecclesiastical choirs and the theatres was supplemented by others from the opera house is not certain. Whatever the precise numbers, this would have been the largest performing group that Handel ever directed in London, and indeed probably the largest assembled in London during his lifetime.

SOME PRACTICAL CONSIDERATIONS
i) The Chorus Parts
On *The King shall rejoice* (which may have been the first anthem to be composed), Handel specified numbers of voices: twelve for the Soprano (treble) part, and seven each for Alto 1, Alto 2, Tenor, Bass 1 and Bass 2. These were clearly round numbers: each section had a leading named singer from the Chapel Royal with six chorus singers in support. The arrangement reflects two things: that the anthems were conceived as essentially choral pieces, and that the distribution reflected contemporary circumstances in London's ecclesiastic choirs, in which (male) altos and basses (in practice, mainly baritones) were the preponderant voices. At various places in the autographs, however, Handel added the names of solo singers, probably with the following practical intentions:

Let thy hand be strengthened
No. 1 b.26 Bass
Two soloists for the opening phrase, perhaps to balance a lighter texture in the voices above, followed by 'tutti Bassi' at b. 28; no indications in the upper voices.

The King shall rejoice
No. 5 b.54 Bass 1
A soloist to strengthen the Tenor line.

My heart is inditing
No. 1 b.22, Alto 1; b.24 Bass 1
Two soloists for each line, probably to secure good opening entries. (At the following entries the Soprano part is marked 'all' and there is no indication for soloists on the Tenor part.)
No. 3 b.35, Bass 1
Two soloists, a similar context to that in *Let thy hand be strengthened*. The entry at b.43 is marked 'all the Basses', with no indication for the Alto and Tenor voices.

Handel's practice was probably dictated by the potential difficulties of ensemble and communication posed by his large performing group, disposed in galleries which did not allow a modern-style focus on a conductor. If the choral group is large, it may be appropriate to treat some passages in a semi-chorus manner, but in other circumstances this may not be necessary.

Provided there is a sufficiency of voices to preserve the choral nature of these anthems, and effective balance is maintained when an orchestrally-accompanied performance is involved, the anthems can be effectively performed by a relatively modest force of singers. In this case some attention needs to be paid to the balance between the voices, taking into account Handel's original SAATBB vocal scoring, and this should be borne in mind if division in the Alto and Bass voices is impractical. Sometimes the division applies only to the occasional chord, or to contexts where, for example, Handel diverted Bass 1 to 'help out' the Tenor part in a way that may not now be required. Preferably the anthems should be performed with as much practical observance of the intentions of Handel's voice-distribution as possible: to take the most famous example, it is a pity to lose the rich spread of sound at the choir entry in *Zadok the Priest*. If, however, performance by undivided SATB voices is unavoidable, then the following adaptations are practical:

Let thy hand be strengthened
Alto
No. 1 Sing Alto 1, except Alto 2 b.37 beat 1 to b.44
No. 2 Sing Alto 1, except Alto 2 at the following places: b.13 to b.17 beat 2; b.37 beat 3 to b.39 beat 2; b.44 beat 3 to b.47 beat 2; b.65. At bb.33, 51 and 61 take the Alto 2 note on beat 1.
No. 3 Sing Alto 1, except Alto 2 b.34 beat 4 to b.37 beat 1, and b.45 beat 3 to b.46.

Zadok the Priest
Alto
Sing Alto 1 throughout, and Soprano 2 if necessary in No. 3 b.22 beat 4 to b.25
Bass
Sing Bass 2 throughout

The King shall rejoice
Alto
No. 1 Sing Alto 1 throughout
No. 3 Sing Alto 2 bb.1-5, Alto 1 bb.6-7
No. 4 Sing Alto 1 to b.75, moving to Alto 2 on beat 3 of that bar. The Alto 2 part from b.70 (beat 2) should be taken by the Tenors, who return to the Tenor part at b.79.
No. 5 Sing Alto 1, except Alto 2 at the following places: b.24 beat 2 to b.26 beat 2; b.31 beat 3 to b.35; b.38; b.70 beat 3 to b.71
Bass
Nos. 1, 3 and 4 Sing Bass 2
No. 5 Sing Bass 1 to b.8, moving to Bass 2 on beat 3; sing Bass 1 b.38 beat 4 and b.39, then return to Bass 2

My heart is inditing
Alto
No. 1 Sing Alto 1 from b.73, then Alto 2 from b.89
No. 2 Sing Alto 1. (In bb.22-28, Alto 1 doubles Soprano and Alto 2 doubles Tenor: either may be followed.)
No. 3 Sing Alto 1, except Alto 2 from b.61 to b.70 beat 2, and from b.78 onwards
No. 4 Sing Alto 2, moving to Alto 1 at b.20 beat 4. Then sing Alto 1, except at the following places: b.44-49 beat 3; b.61; b.68 beat 2 onwards. The Alto 2 phrase in bb.25-26 should be taken by the Tenors.

In the final movements of *Let thy hand be strengthened* and *The King shall rejoice* Handel used an Italian convention of vowel elision whereby, on the repetition of the word 'alleluia', the first and last syllables were merged into a single vowel sound. Occurrences of this are indicated thus:

'al-le-lu-ia, al-le-lu-ia'

There are also places where, conversely, Handel intended a clear articulation of separate notes within a single vowel sound, as for example at b.16 of the final movement of *The King shall rejoice*, and the soprano part at bar 3 of the last movement of *Let thy hand be strengthened*. In a very few cases it is not clear whether Handel intended such an articulation or simply forgot to add a tie: in Alto 2 at b.36 of the final movement of *Let thy hand be strengthened* the repetition was probably intended, but the application at bar 64 of the final movement of *My heart is inditing* is less certain.

Handel's indications of trills in the vocal parts have been retained, and supplemented by some editorial suggestions. Choral trills should be sung lightly, and their inclusion may not be appropriate in performances by very large choirs.

ii) Alterations to rhythms and notes
Unless otherwise noted, Handel's rhythmic notation is preserved throughout, and editorial suggestions for rhythmic modification are indicated by rhythmic 'flags'. It seems to have been the case that rhythms in some places were sharpened in performance, and/or brought into general conformity to the prevailing rhythmic patterns of the movement, though the degree of regimentation is uncertain.

A special case is presented by No. 2 of *The King shall rejoice*, where Handel's varied notation of dotted rhythms is found in conjunction with passages of triplets: they are in direct conjunction at bb.95-97. In practice, string players usually have no difficulty in integrating the sprung, slightly over-dotted rhythm which is implied from the opening of the movement with the triplets. The opening choral entry at bb.21-22 seems, however, to be intentionally notated in even quavers. Most choirs will find it easier (and more effective) to match their rhythms to the orchestra at the cadences in bb.44-46, 72-75 and 98-99.

In addition to some inconsistencies of rhythm between voices and instruments, there are a few clashes of pitches, mainly at cadences. Some of these are of little practical consequence and can easily be brought into conformity, if desired, but others may be the result of unintentional errors on Handel's part. (If he laid down the basso continuo and vocal lines first and then filled in the orchestral element, he may well have covered over the voice parts on his large autograph score in the act of writing the instrumental parts.) The inconsistencies do not reflect a general carelessness on Handel's part about details in the composition of the score, and the few cases in question may well have been amended in the part-books at the rehearsals: no original performing material survives from the 1727 coronation. Editorial amendments and suggestions are elucidated in footnotes to the music and in the textual commentary.

iii) The Continuo

A special organ was constructed for the 1727 coronation, apparently located in the galleries that were specially constructed for the musicians, and probably needed because Westminster Abbey's own organ was not at the pitch of the orchestral instruments. Handel may have directed from the organ but it seems more likely, in view of the size and dispersal of the performers, that he would have given his full attention to directing the performances and entrusted the organ playing to someone else. There is no mention of the harpsichord on the scores or in contemporary reports: it would probably have been regarded as musically superfluous, and taking up valuable space. Since there are no movements for soloists in the anthems, the need for the conventional continuo role is very limited, though the presence of at least one chord-playing instrument is desirable. Performances using organ alone, harpsichord alone, or both together, are possible within the style of the period. The keyboard realisation provided with the hire material for this edition can be taken by a single instrument or adapted for two players when both harpsichord and organ are employed. The 'Organo' stave at the opening of *Zadok the Priest* conforms to the way that the instrument was used in Handel's oratorio choruses: the organ accompanies 'soft' during the orchestral prelude, and then changes to 'loud' (probably basically doubling the voices) at the choral entry.[2] (The 'soft' at the opening is therefore a specific direction for the organ, and not a general dynamic mark.) In practice it is not difficult to combine this style in the use of the organ with the simple fulfilment of the conventional continuo filling-in role when required.

SOURCES

i) Principal manuscript source

A British Library, RM 20.h.5. Handel's composition score of the anthems; he did not date the manuscript, though he added 'Fine' after each anthem except *Zadok the Priest*. The anthems are now bound in the order 2, 1, 3, 4; no two anthems are associated by conjunct paper-gatherings. The first leaf of *Let thy hand be strengthened* (f.11) is in the hand of John Christopher Smith the younger, and was probably copied in the late 1750s to replace the original leaf which had become lost or damaged: this may have been at the time the front leaf of the anthem autograph. For the music on this leaf (bb.1-25 of the anthem) we therefore do not have Handel's autograph. On f. 34v the same copyist, and probably at the same period, also filled in the score of one passage in *The King shall rejoice* No. 5 (bb.59-65) that Handel had left incomplete with a cue to repeat a previous passage (bb.8-14). The autograph also has various other additions in the hands of Handel and of John Christopher Smith the elder, relating to the re-use of movements from the anthems in Handel's oratorios, but not relevant to the Coronation Anthems themselves.[3] Since the relevant portions of the autograph may have been temporarily removed in connection with the use of the music elsewhere, it is unlikely that the present order of the anthems is significant. The manuscript probably did not have a permanent binding during Handel's lifetime.

ii) Secondary manuscript sources

Because of the popularity of the Coronation Anthems there are many surviving manuscript sources from the eighteenth and nineteenth centuries, many of them of little value for casting light on the music texts of the anthems or Handel's performances. The following manuscript scores were copied within a couple of decades of 1727:

B Manchester Public Library, Henry Watson Music Library, MS 130 Hd4 vol. 49. From the Aylesford Collection, originally copied for Charles Jennens c. 1732.[4] Copyist S2.

C Fitzwilliam Museum, Cambridge, MU MS 812. From the Barrett Lennard Collection, copied c.1740. Copyist J. C. Smith the elder. Order of anthems: 1, 3, 2, 4.[5]

D Hampshire Record Office, Winchester, Gerald Coke Handel Collection. From the Shaftesbury Collection, copied c.1740-5. Copyists S1 and S5.

E Fitzwilliam Museum, Cambridge, MU MS 813. From the Barrett Lennard Collection, a volume perhaps originally intended for the Granville Collection, copied c.1740-5. Copyists S1 and S5.

F British Library RM 19.g.1a. From the Smith Collection, copied in the 1740s. Copyist S5.

G Royal College of Music, London, MS 892. From the collection of Sir John Dolben, probably copied in the 1740s. Order of anthems 2, 4, 1, 3.

Two other copies may be of similarly early origin:

H Mainz, Collection of B. Schott's Söhne. Possibly copied in the 1730s, and of English origin.

J Austin, Texas, U.S.A., Harry Ransom Humanities Research Center, University of Texas at Austin, Finney Music Collection 10. Formerly the property of the Oxford Musical Society, for whom the score was perhaps originally copied.[6]

The following were probably copied during the 1760s:

K Hamburg, Staats- und Universitätsbibliothek, M C/259. Possibly copied for J. C. Smith the younger in connection with performances at the London theatres. Copyist S5. Order of anthems 1, 3, 4, 2.

L Hamburg, Staats- und Universitätsbibliothek, M B/1661. Copyist James Blackman. Order of anthems 2, 4, 1, 3.

M Massey University, Palmerston North, New Zealand.

iii) Printed editions

N *Handel's Celebrated Coronation Anthems in Score. ... Printed for J. Walsh.* Published c.1743, inaugurating a series of volumes of Handel's church music. Vol. I, as originally published, comprised anthems 2, 4, 1; *The King shall rejoice* appeared in Vol. II, with Handel's Funeral Anthem for Queen Caroline, but Walsh apparently soon re-issued Vol. I with all four Coronation Anthems.

O *Anthem for the Coronation of George II[D]*. Arnold's edition: the four anthems were issued separately with this title page in 1795-6, in the order 1, 2, 4, 3.

Relationship of the sources

It seems certain that an important early manuscript copy of the anthems has been lost, which included a significant correction in *The King shall rejoice* No. 3, bars 4-5. Here Handel wrote 'and worship', with a crotchet for 'and' in the vocal parts at b.4. This has not been amended in the autograph, but at some early stage the rhythm in b.4 was altered to two quavers and an extra word was added, to read 'and great worship'.[7] (This brings the text into slightly closer conformity with Psalm xxi verse 5 as found in the English Prayer Book.) With one exception, all of the secondary sources for the Coronation Anthems – manuscripts and printed editions – have the amended form, and were thus presumably derived, directly or indirectly, from a copy that had that reading. The exception is source **C**, which must have been copied directly from Handel's autograph. **C** is the only copy of the anthems in the hand of J. C. Smith senior, Handel's principal copyist. Nevertheless, several other early copies can be assumed to have been produced under the authority of Handel or Smith, and source **B** (probably the earliest surviving secondary copy) shows that the alteration was an early contribution. It is possible that the amendment was made in Handel's performing score of the anthems, before the first performance in 1727; accordingly, performers have a legitimate choice between the two readings. Most sources present the anthems in the order given in this edition: the variations may be significant, or may merely reflect situations in which the order of the anthems had been temporarily disturbed in a copyist's source. The resemblance in the order of the anthems may suggest that **L** and **N** were derived from **G**, or a common source.

EDITORIAL METHOD

This edition is based on Source **A**, which is mostly clearly written, in spite of amendments made during composition. Apart from the reading from *The King shall rejoice* noted above, the secondary sources provide little useful information to clarify or correct the text from **A**, though they add new errors of their own. Editorial amendments of significance to the performers are presented in footnotes to the vocal score or in the following commentary. *The King shall rejoice* was edited by Damian Cranmer and the remaining three anthems by Donald Burrows: this combined edition has been prepared under the general editorship of Donald Burrows.

Clefs for the vocal parts have been modernised. Handel used C clefs for the upper voices: Soprano (C1), Alto (C2) and Tenor (C3). Handel did not write all of the verbal text under every part, but his intentions are normally unambiguous: any exceptions are noted. Handel's slurs in the vocal part, which indicate text-underlay, have been omitted. The system of accidentals has been modernised: there are very few places where there is any doubt about the correct note. Spelling and punctuation have been modernised and, as for example with 'wemen' and 'strenght', corrected. Movement numbers are editorial. Editorial additions of dynamics, trills, etc., are shown by square brackets, and editorial additions of slurs and ties are indicated by ‿⁀ . Editorial suggestions for rhythmic modification are shown by 'flag' rhythms above the stave: these include suggestions for shortening the final notes of some phrases, to conform to harmonic changes in the orchestral parts. The hemiola cadential rhythmic re-grouping in triple time is indicated by horizontal square brackets thus: ⌐⎯⎤ ⌐⎯⎤ ⌐⎯⎤ .

The keyboard accompaniment is a practical reduction of the principal activity of the orchestral parts, and does not pretend to include all elements of the texture: variations in the orchestral scoring are indicated above the stave. The scoring for each movement is given at the beginning, to assist with the planning of orchestral rehearsals: in addition, the participation of a continuo instrument, and of bassoons in the basso part where not separately specified, is to be assumed. Trills from the orchestral parts are indicated, but may not always be practical on the keyboard. Editorial continuo realisation is distinguished from orchestral reduction by the use of small-size notes. The harmonic bass line is preserved at the correct pitch as the lowest part of the accompaniment. Passages for continuo written by Handel in the alto or soprano clefs are indicated by 'Cont': these often double the violin parts. Variations in scoring of the bass line, shown by Handel by the use of the tenor clef or by specific cues, are indicated by 'senza Cb' and 'tutti', to indicate the presence or absence of '16 foot' tone.

TEXTUAL NOTES
All listed readings relate to Source **A**, unless otherwise noted, and all singers' names quoted were written in **A** by Handel.

Let thy hand be strengthened
Handel wrote biblical text-references above the start of his other three anthems, but the first page of his autograph for this anthem is lost and any similar heading is not preserved in the secondary copies. **C**, which was probably copied from the autograph before the leaf was lost, does not reproduce Handel's headings: Smith wrote 'Coronation Anthems', to which another hand has added 'For King George 2^d'. On **A** Smith the younger's title is 'Anthems [space] for the Coronation of his Majesty King George the 2^d'.
No. 1
bar
1-25 **C** has been taken as the copy-text for these bars, since it probably is a more accurate transcription of Handel's lost original than that now found in **A**, which omits the Allegro marking.

26 B: 'Wh[eely] et Bell'. Samuel Weely and Thomas Bell were singers from the Chapel Royal. Since the autograph of the previous bar is missing, it is possible that Handel also added singers' names to the preceding entry in A and T, though this is unlikely since he wrote 'tutti Bassi' at b.28 but nothing against the other parts.

27 Handel made a clear distinction between passages where 'strengthened' was to be treated as two or three syllables.

63 B: Handel wrote the beginning of the word again at beat 1, an error at a change of stave-system.

No. 2
1 The upper instrumental part is not labelled, but the participation of the oboes with the violins is indicated by his direction 'H[autboy] colla voce' at b.45.

13 B: Handel wrote 'Mr Wh. Bell' against an initially-intended entry on beat 3, and then deleted the names. If this anthem were the last to be composed, this might suggest that Handel had decided against the use of solo voices at some of the entries elsewhere.

16 Bc figuring $\frac{4}{2}$ on beat 1, but it probably applied to the original note g, which Handel subsequently altered to f.

31 A, T: Handel did not add slurs to clarify the word-setting here: possibly A1 should move with S.

69 Voices and Bc written as a dotted minim by Handel. No direction for Obs, who were perhaps intended to rejoin Vlns for the closing ritornello.

Zadok the Priest
Handel's heading: 'Anthem 1 Kings 1.48' (*sic*)
No. 1
1 Handel's 'soft' applies to the organ stave only: the scoring of Obs and Bsns militates against a very quiet opening.

30 Handel wrote pause signs over the rests in the vocal parts, but not elsewhere: these may in any case have been added in connection with the later uses of the music.

No. 2
Handel wrote 'out' in pencil above the first page, but this refers to the later use of the other movements for oratorio performances, and not to the Coronation Anthem.

No. 3
3 Handel originally wrote an extra bar, repeating the music of bar 3 to the text 'Long live the King', but then deleted the bar.

49	Handel wrote separate staves for B1 and B2 throughout the anthem: at beat 4 B2 has f and B1 has d, the latter probably an error.
58	Handel indicated the Adagio on beat 3, but a slight preceding *rallentando* may be implied.

The King shall rejoice

Handel's heading: ' ψ [i.e. Psalm] 21. v. i. et v. 3'. Before the beginning of the score he added specifications for the vocal parts, incorporating the names of the section leaders from the Chapel Royal: S: 'C[anto]' 12; A1: 'H[ughes] et 6'; A2: 'Freem[an] et 6'; T: 'Church et 6'; B1: 'Wheely et 6'; B2: 'Gates et 6'. These were repeated on the following pages of the score and at the beginning of No. 3.

No. 1

34	B: Last note a in B1, c′ in B2. B1 is probably an error comparable to that in *Zadok the Priest* No. 3 b.49, but in this case it may also be connected with a re-drafting of the melody in S.
44	S: see footnote to this bar. There would be a good case for altering S to conform to the melody as in Vln 1: compare A at bars 61, 67.
63	A: the third note was clearly written by Handel as f′ in both A1 and A2.

No. 2

1	Handel indicated a division of violins into three sections for this movement, with Vln. 3 doubling Vla.
75	A: note repetition is clear in **A**. On beats 2-3, A melody is supported by '4 3' figuring, but in Vln. 3/Vla Handel wrote dotted crotchet a, quaver b, probably in error.
93-94	A: no word-underlay in **A**. Several early copies (including **B, C, D, E**) have 'exceeding glad', but 'glad shall he be' is implied by S and B.
111	Some copies introduce *piano* b.111 note 2, and *forte* at b.113 note 2.

No. 3

1	Handel wrote *non tanto allegro* above Vln 1, *a tempo giusto* above Vln 2 and below Bc: none of these is deleted. Smith copied only *a tempo giusto* in **C**.
5	A1: Handel wrote two notes, f′ and c″ for both chords: Smith copied only c″ in **C**.

No. 4

Handel wrote 'blessing' in some places, 'blessings' in others.

17-21	A2: Handel also wrote an additional alternative part: see the footnote to the music.
50	Bc figuring '7 6' on beats 2-3 and the melody follows this in Ob. 2, clashing with other parts: probably an idea that was abandoned by Handel, but not corrected.

No. 5

9, 60	Bc figuring '7 6' at beats 1-2, but this does not conform to the harmony above.
54	B1: 'Whely' written by Handel at note 2. No word-underlay is given and the quavers on beats 3-4 are beamed as four, but the soloist was perhaps intended to sing 'alleluia' to match the Tenor part.
59-65	Mainly left as empty staves above the Bc part by Handel, with a cue to repeat the parallel passage from bb. 8-14.
67-71	Handel wrote the final bars of the movement on a leaf that had a discarded earlier sketch from the movement.[8]

My heart is inditing

Handel's heading: ' ψ [i.e. Psalm]. 45 v. 1.10.12 49 v. 23' (*sic*)

No. 1

22, 24	'Mr Wheely Mr Bell' next to B at b.22, 'Mr Hughs Mr Lee' next to A at b.24; also repeated as 'H & L' at bar 63 (A), 'W. G' at b.64 (B)
44-45	Handel wrote 'pian' twice: it is not clear if one was intended to apply to Obs, or both referred to the string parts.
67	B: no dot, or rest, after minim
73	'tutti' next to Bc at beat 3: this is probably an indication for the organ, relating to the chorus entry.
78	B: see footnote to music. Handel probably forgot to amend this to conform to B2.
94	T: third note clearly f′, but perhaps a′ intended.

No. 2

There are no indications for solo singers in this movement. At some places Handel spread 'were' as if two syllables were intended, but this is not confirmed by his arrangement of the notes.

28	S: Handel altered the first note of beat 3 from g′ to b′
41:	B: at the second note Handel clearly wrote g, though e in Bc. At beats 3-4 S and T clash with Vlns, and editorial alternatives are suggested.

No. 3

Handel's scoring of the movement at the opening is for Vlns without Obs, but Handel indicated Obs *colla parte* with S at bar 22.

34	B: 'Mr W[heely] & B[ell] ', followed by 'all the Basses' at b. 43. No indications in A and T.
44	Vla: f′ beat 2, in error for g′
50	A2: beat 3 may have been an accidental error; Vla doubling voice has crotchet e′.

69	A2, T: final noteheads ambiguous, but probably altered from e′ to f′ (A2) and from c′ to d′ (T).
82	S, Vln 1: conflicting rhythm beat 3, see footnote to music.

No. 4

1	Handel wrote *allegro* at the top of the score and above Vln stave; also *allegro e staccato* below Bc, with 'staccato' positioned so that it clearly refers to the crotchets from beat 3 onwards.
6	Bc: figurings '7 6' on b. 1 and b.3, probably an idea from the drafting stage and not followed through in the final orchestral harmony.
25	Handel wrote 'Violin Piano' at b.3; this direction has been moved editorially, and applied to all orchestral parts.
50	A1: beat 1 altered by Handel from quavers e♯′, g♯′, though this reading was retained in copies, including C.
56/57	Vln 3: b.56 beat 4 first note a′; b. 57 beat 4 first note c″. Probably accidental errors by Handel: in these bars Vln 3 is otherwise in unison with Ob. 1, Ob. 2 and Vln 1/2, all of which were fully written out by Handel and have c″ and e″, respectively.
64	A2 and orchestra: no accidental to final quaver. The parts for Obs and Vlns suggest that g′ natural is more likely, though it is possible that Handel assumed g♯′ (and equivalent in the orchestral parts) on this beat.

ACKNOWLEDGMENTS

The editors thank the owners and keepers of the relevant library collections for access to the sources for the anthems; we are particularly grateful to those who arranged to provide films or photographic copies of sources that are in collections outside Great Britain. For technical assistance in the preparation of this edition, we thank Blaise Compton and Rosemary Kingdon.

Donald Burrows
July 2002

1   For details of the historical events relating to the Coronation Anthems, see Donald Burrows, 'Handel and the 1727 Coronation', *Musical Times* cxviii (1977), pp. 469-473, and the subsequent letter on p. 725.

2   In the oratorios the organ normally played the bass line *tasto solo* in 'soft' passages, while the harpsichord played the continuo chords: Handel's figured bass indicates that the organ should play chords in No. 1 of *Zadok the Priest*.

3   See the entry for the autograph in Donald Burrows and Martha J. Ronish, *A Catalogue of Handel's Musical Autographs* (Oxford, 1994), pp. 212-213.

4   For the various collections of eighteenth-century scores, see: Terence Best (ed.) *Handel Collections and their History* (Oxford, 1993) [for the Aylesford, Barrett Lennard and Shaftesbury Collections]; Donald Burrows, 'The "Granville" and "Smith"

Collections of Handel manuscripts' in Chris Banks, Arthur Searle and Malcolm Turner (eds.) *Sundry Sorts of Music Books* (London, 1993), pp. 231-247; Donald Burrows, 'Sir John Dolben, Musical Patron' and 'Sir John Dolben's music collection', *Musical Times* cxx (1979), pp. 65-67, 149-151. For the music copyists, see Jens Peter Larsen, *Handel's "Messiah"* (London, 1957)

5   The order of the anthems is only recorded when it differs from that of the present edition.

6   See David Hunter, 'The Oxford Musical Society's manuscript of Handel's Coronation Anthems at Texas', *Newsletter of the American Handel Society* xi/1 (April 1996), pp. 1, 3, 5.

7   Walsh's edition gives the two quavers, but only the single word 'great' as text.

8   See Burrows and Ronish, *op. cit.*, p. 213, note to f. 35.

LET THY HAND BE STRENGTHENED

LET THY HAND BE STRENGTHENED

Psalm lxxxix, 13

No. 1   Chorus   LET THY HAND BE STRENGTHENED

* The opening entries for A, T and B (bb. 25 - 27) may be sung by semi-chorus.
Handel marked the opening Bass entry for two singers, with 'Tutti Bassi' at b. 28.

4

Senza Cb.

6

- alt - - - ed.

Psalm lxxxix, 14

No. 2 Chorus LET JUSTICE AND JUDGMENT

* Handel wrote 'thy' for 'the' throughout the movement.

38

mer - cy and truth ____ go, go be - fore thy

go, ____ go ____ be - fore thy

mer - cy and truth ____ go, go be - fore ____ thy

go, go be - fore thy

mer - cy and truth go, go be - fore thy

43

face, let mer - cy let mer - cy and truth ____ go ____

face, let mer - cy and truth

face, let mer - cy, let mer - cy and truth

face, let mer - cy, and truth

face, let mer - cy and truth, ____ and truth

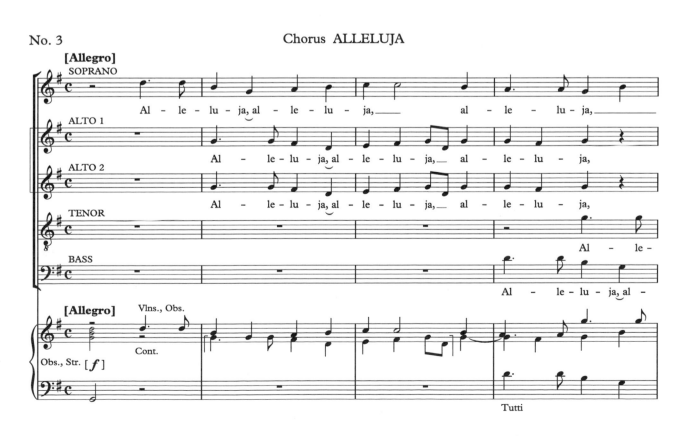

No. 3   Chorus ALLELUJA

20

Tutti

al – le – – lu – ja,_____
– le – lu – – ja,_____
– le – lu – ja,_____
– ja,_____
– ja,_____

____ al – le – lu – ja, al – le – lu – ja.
____ al – le – lu – ja, al – le – lu – ja.
____ al – le – lu – ja, al – le – lu – ja.
____ al – le – lu – ja, al – le – lu – ja.
____ al – le – lu – ja, al – le – lu – ja.

Adagio

Adagio

ZADOK THE PRIEST

ZADOK THE PRIEST

I Kings i, 39-40

No. 1   Chorus ZADOK THE PRIEST

[Orchestral bass continues in quaver rhythm]

No. 2   Chorus AND ALL THE PEOPLE REJOIC'D

No. 3   Chorus GOD SAVE THE KING

34

God save the King, long live the King. May the King live,

God save the King, long live the King. May the King live,

God save the King, long live the King. May the King live,

God save the King, long live the King. May the King live,

God save the King, long live the King. May the King live,

may the King live for e - - ver, for e - ver, for e - ver, a - men,

may the King live for e - - ver, for e - - ver, a - men,

may the King live for e - - ver, for e - - ver, a - men,

may the King live for e - - ver, for e - ver, for e - ver, a - men,

may the King live for e - - ver, for e - ver, for e - ver, a - men,

* Last beat of b.49, Handel wrote f for Bass 2 and d for Bass 1: the latter was almost certainly an error.

THE KING SHALL REJOICE

THE KING SHALL REJOICE

Psalm xxi,1

No. 1   Chorus THE KING SHALL REJOICE

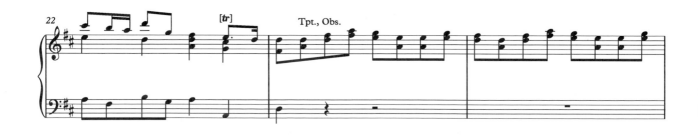

46

* The last two notes in this bar of the autograph are obliterated by crossing out. Handel has indicated 'd c' above the notes, though these clash with the accompaniment. The rhythm is given here as it appears in early copies, but Handel may have intended: See Preface and Textual Notes.

strength O ___ Lord, the King shall re-joice in thy strength O Lord,

strength O ___ Lord, the King shall re-joice in thy strength O Lord,

strength O ___ Lord, the King shall re-joice in thy strength O Lord,

strength O Lord, the King shall re-joice in thy strength O Lord,

C

in thy strength O Lord, the King ___ shall re-joice, ___

in thy strength O Lord, the King shall re-joice, ___

in thy strength O Lord, the King shall re-joice, ___

in thy strength O Lord, the King ___ shall re-joice, ___

C

-joice in thy strength O Lord.

-joice in thy strength O____ Lord.

-joice in thy strength O Lord.

-joice in thy strength O Lord.

Tpts., Obs.

Tutti

Psalm xxi,1

No. 2   Chorus EXCEEDING GLAD SHALL HE BE

52

*Some adjustments to the chorus rhythm may be necessary in this movement, to fit with the accompaniment. See Preface.

54

58

*Handel wrote 'in'.

glad, ex - ceed - ing glad shall he be

- - - tion, glad shall he be

- - - - - - - - - tion,

glad, ex - ceed - ing glad shall he be

of thy sal - - - va - - -

of thy sal - - - va - - -

of thy sal - - va - - -

of thy sal - - va - - -

- - - tion, of thy sal - va - tion.

- - - tion, of thy sal - va - tion.

- - - tion, of thy sal - va - tion.

- - - tion, of thy sal - va - tion.

62

Chorus GLORY AND GREAT WORSHIP

No. 3

*Handel's autograph has crotchets for vocal parts and omits 'great': the alternative, found in other sources, may have been a pre-performance revision.

Psalm xxi,3

No. 4

Chorus THOU HAST PREVENTED HIM

senza Cb.

64

*Handel's autograph has an alternative Alto 2 part [♩ ♩ 𝄽] followed by 3 bars rest.
good – ness

bless - ings, with the bless - ings of

thou hast pre -

good - - - ness, thou hast pre -

- ings of _____ good - ness

good - ness with the bless - ings ___ of ___

thou hast pre - vent - ed him with the bless - ings of

- vent - - - - - ed him with the bless - ings of

No. 5

Chorus ALLELUIA

senza Bassi

78

*Handel's autograph indicates that this part was taken by a soloist, the other voices joining Bass 2. The soloist may have been intended to sing the text of the Tenor part.

MY HEART IS INDITING OF A GOOD MATTER

MY HEART IS INDITING
OF A GOOD MATTER

Psalm xlv, 1

No. 1   Chorus MY HEART IS INDITING

* bb. 22–73 may be taken by a semi-chorus: see Preface.

made un-to the King, which I have made un-to the King.

made un-to the King, which I have made un-to the King.

My

Bar 78, Bass: Handel also wrote ![notation] for Bass 1, but probably forgot to correct this.

Psalm xlv, 10

No. 2   Chorus KINGS' DAUGHTERS WERE AMONG
THY HONOURABLE WOMEN

104

* Suggested editorial alternatives in small notes.

Psalm xlv, 10,12

No. 3   Chorus   UPON THY RIGHT HAND DID STAND THE QUEEN

bb. 22–42 may be taken by a semi-chorus: see Preface.

106

the King shall have plea - sure in __ thy __ beau - ty.

the King shall have plea - sure in thy beau - ty.

the King shall have plea - sure in thy beau - ty.

the King shall have plea - sure in thy beau - ty.

the King shall have plea - sure in thy beau - ty.

Up - on __ thy right __ hand did stand the

Up - on __ thy right __ hand did stand the

Up - on thy right hand did stand the

Up - on thy right hand did stand __ the

Up - on __ thy right hand did stand __ the

senza Cb.

Tutti

Bar 82: at beat 3 Handel wrote ♪♪♪ in Violin 1 but ♪♪♪ in the Soprano part.

the King shall have plea-sure in___ thy___ beau - ty.

the King shall have plea-sure in___ thy beau - ty.

the King shall have plea-sure in___ thy beau - ty.

the King shall have plea-sure in_____ thy beau - ty.

the King shall have plea-sure in thy beau - ty.

[f]

Isaiah xlix, 23

No. 4   Chorus KINGS SHALL BE THY NURSING FATHERS

Bar 1: Handel wrote *Allegro e staccato* against the Basso part.

116

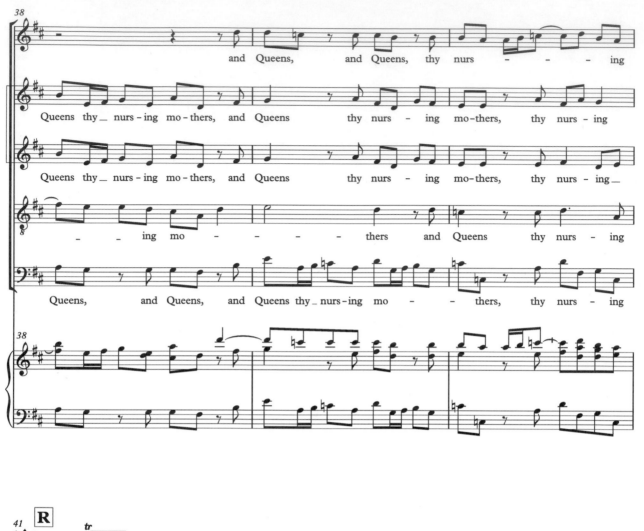

120

fa - - - - - - thers, shall be thy nurs - ing

nurs - ing fa - - - - thers, shall be thy nurs - ing

nurs - ing fa - - - - thers, shall be thy nurs - ing

nurs - ing fa - - - - thers, shall be thy nurs - ing

nurs - ing fa - - - - thers, shall be thy nurs - ing

fa - - thers, and Queens, and Queens thy nurs - - ing

fa - - thers, and Queens, and Queens thy nurs - - ing

fa - - thers, and Queens, and Queens thy nurs - - ing

fa - - thers, and Queens, and Queens thy nurs - - ing

fa - - thers, and Queens, and Queens thy nurs - - ing

NOVELLO REVISED STANDARD CHORAL EDITIONS

Fully revised and edited performing versions of many of the major works in the large-scale choral concert repertoire, replacing the standard Novello editions, often putting back the composers' intentions, restoring the original text, modernised accompaniments and providing new English translations.
Orchestral material, where necessary, is available on hire.

J.S. BACH
(ed. Neil Jenkins)
Christmas Oratorio
NOV072500
German and English text
Magnificats in D & E♭
NOV072529
German and English text in the four Lauds in the E♭ version
Mass in B minor NOV078430
St. John Passion
NOV072489
German and English text
St. Matthew Passion
NOV072478
German and English text

BEETHOVEN
(ed. Michael Pilkington)
Choral Finale to the Ninth Symphony
NOV072490
German and English text
Mass in C
NOV078560
Missa Solemnis (Mass in D)
NOV072497

BRAHMS
(Pilkington)
A German Requiem
NOV072492
German and English text

DVOŘÁK
(Pilkington)
Mass in D NOV072491
Requiem NOV072516
Stabat Mater NOV072503
Te Deum NOV078573

ELGAR
(ed. Bruce Wood)
The Dream of Gerontius
NOV072530
Great Is the Lord
NOV078595

GOUNOD
(Pilkington)
Messe solennelle de Sainte Cécile
NOV072495

HANDEL
Belshazzar
(ed. Donald Burrows) NOV070530
Four Coronation Anthems
NOV072507
 The King Shall Rejoice
 (ed. Damian Cranmer)
 Let Thy Hand be Strengthened
 (Burrows)
 My Heart is Inditing *(Burrows)*
 Zadok the Priest *(Burrows)*
Judas Maccabaeus
(ed. Merlin Channon)
NOV072486
The King Shall Rejoice
(Cranmer) NOV072496
Messiah
(ed. Watkins Shaw) NOV070137
 Study Score NOV890031
O Praise the Lord
(from Chandos Anthem No. 9)
(ed. Grayston Beeks) NOV072511
This Is the Day
(ed. Hurley) NOV072510
Zadok the Priest
(Burrows) NOV290704

HAYDN
(ed. Pilkington)
The Creation
NOV072485
German and English text
The Seasons
NOV072493
German and English text
Te Deum Laudamus
NOV078463
"Maria Theresa" Mass
NOV078474
Mass "In Time of War"
NOV072514
"Nelson" Mass
NOV072513
Harmoniemesse
NOV078507

MAUNDER
Olivet to Calvary
NOV072487

MENDELSSOHN
(Pilkington)
Elijah
NOV070201
German and English text

Hymn of Praise
NOV072506

MOZART
Requiem
(ed. Duncan Druce) NOV070529
Coronation Mass
(Mass in C K.317)
(Pilkington) NOV072505
Mass in C minor
(reconstr. Philip Wilby) NOV078452

PURCELL
Come, Ye Sons of Art, Away
(Wood) NOV072467
Welcome to All the Pleasures
(Wood) NOV290674
Ed. Vol. 15 Royal Welcome Songs 1
(Wood) NOV151102
Ed. Vol. 22A Catches
(ed. Ian Spink) NOV151103

ROSSINI
(Pilkington)
Petite messe solennelle
NOV072436

SCHUBERT
Mass in G, D.167 (SSA version)
NOV070258

SCHÜTZ
(Jenkins)
Christmas Story
NOV072525
German and English text

STAINER
(ed. Pilkington)
The Crucifixion
NOV072488

VERDI
(Pilkington)
Requiem
NOV072403

VIVALDI
(ed. Jasmin Cameron)
Gloria
NOV078441